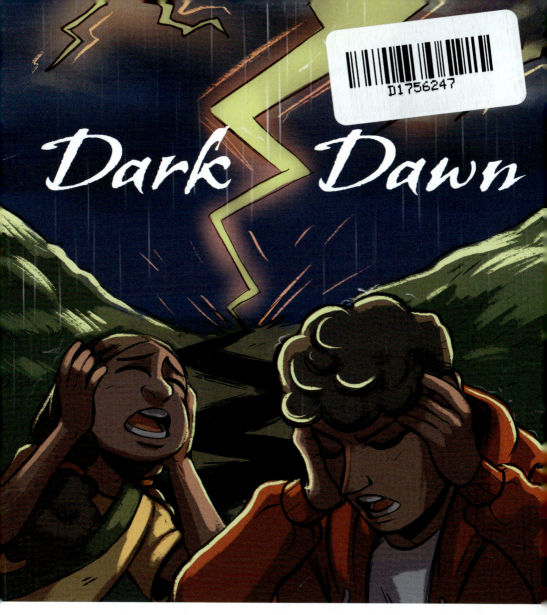

Dark Dawn

Written by Danny Pearson

Illustrated by Markia Jenai

Collins

1 Dark storm

Flynn finished his breakfast. The day was getting hot.

Come on, Sam. Let's look around.

The siblings set off across the campsite.

Don't be long!

Flynn and Sam headed up a hill.

First one to the top wins!

4

They didn't stop until they had reached the summit.

Look!

What on Earth is that?

A dark shape started to form in the clouds overhead.

The wind was wild. It was as dark as night.

Stay away!

The monster opened its mouth.

I was a servant of Grim. He plans to end the world. This crystal holds his power. I escaped with it.

Claw gave Sam the crystal.

Claw pointed to a cave.

Follow the pyramid symbol. It leads to the abyss. Throw the crystal into the abyss to stop Grim.

A colossal shape appeared from the storm.

I am Grim.
Hand me that
crystal, girl.

Never!

15

16

Claw ran at Grim.

But Grim had too much power. The wind hit Claw, throwing him to the ground.

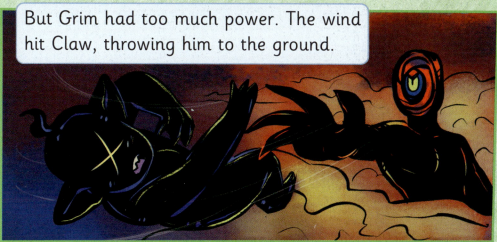

Claw vanished.

Flynn and Sam ran until they reached the cave. The wind lashed around them.

Sam held up her torch.

The pyramid symbol! It will take us to the abyss.

19

3 The abyss

As they reached the abyss, Flynn and Sam heard footsteps approaching. They were trapped.

Now, hand me that crystal, girl!

Sam threw her bag.

Take it!

Flynn froze.

Grim's servants jumped for the bag.

23

Sam threw the crystal into the abyss.

Grim's servants leapt after it. Head first, they fell into the dark.

Sam and Flynn saw light and heard birds singing ahead.

They crawled into the sunshine.